# Ladders
# Under the Sea

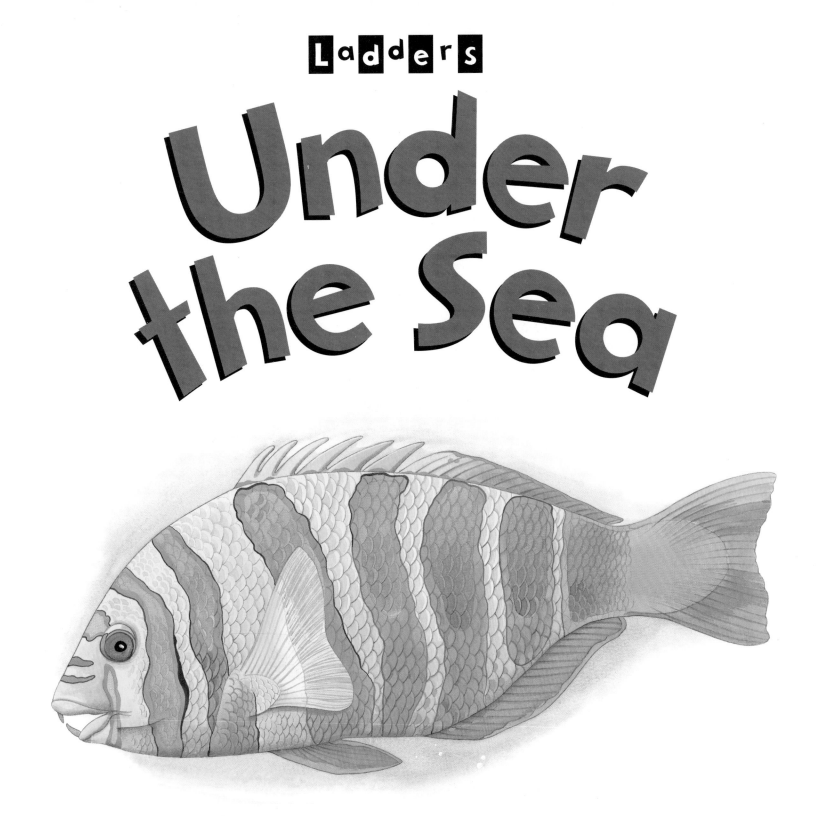

World Book

in association with

TWOCAN

**Written by:** Angela Wilkes
**Story by:** Belinda Webster
**Consultants:** Dr. Iram Siraj-Blatchford, Institute of Education, London; Dr. Frances Dipper
**Editors:** Sarah Fecher and Deborah Kespert
**Art director:** Belinda Webster
**Design:** Alex Frampton
**Main illustrations:** Steve Holmes
**Computer illustrations:** Jon Stuart
**U.S. editor:** Sharon Nowakowski, World Book Publishing

First published in the United States and Canada by
World Book, Inc.
525 W. Monroe
Chicago, IL 60661
in association with Two-Can Publishing, Ltd.

**For information on other World Book products, call 1-800-255-1750, x2238,
or visit our Web site at http://www.worldbook.com**

© Two-Can Publishing Ltd, 1998

**Library of Congress Cataloging-in-Publication Data**
Under the sea.
    p.   cm. — (Ladders)
    Includes index.
    Summary: Gives information about some of the animals that live in the sea; includes
    a short story and several picture puzzles relating to underwater life.
      ISBN 0-7166-7705-9 (hc).  —  ISBN 0-7166-7706-7 (sc)
      1. Marine animals—Juvenile literature.  [1. Marine animals.]  I. Series
QL122.2.U54    1998
591.77--dc21                                                    97-44143

**Photographic credits:** p5: Bruce Coleman Ltd; p6: Tony Stone Images; p8: BBC Natural History Unit;
p9: Tony Stone Images; p10: Natural History Photographic Agency; p11: Planet Earth Pictures;
p12: Tony Stone Images; p17: Planet Earth Pictures; p18: Planet Earth Pictures; p19: Tony Stone Images;
p20: Oxford Scientific Films; p22: Planet Earth Pictures; p23: Tony Stone Images.

Printed and bound in Spain

(hc) 1 2 3 4 5 6 7 8 9 10 02 01 00 99 98
(sc) 1 2 3 4 5 6 7 8 9 10 02 01 00 99 98

# What's inside?

This book tells you about lots of exciting animals that live under the sea. In this strange underwater world, animals can breathe in the water, some swim all day, and others crawl among rocks and plants on the seabed.

# Dolphin and whale

Dolphins and whales are similar animals that live in the ocean. They are mammals, not fish. They feed their young with milk produced by the mother. They also swim up to the surface to breathe, then dive below with a splash.

Smooth, rubbery **skin** helps a blue whale glide through the water.

A **baby whale** swims close to its mother for safety.

To swim, a whale flips its powerful **tail** up and down.

## It's a fact!

A newborn blue whale weighs as much as a grown elephant. A grown blue whale is as long as a row of five elephants!

4

A whale breathes by sucking in air through one or two **blowholes** on top of its head.

When a whale breathes out, a **spout** of misty spray shoots high into the sky.

A blue whale has a giant **mouth** but eats only the tiniest animals in the sea.

Small, crusty shellfish, called **barnacles**, live on a whale's back.

Dolphins often play together. They swim in groups and make clicking sounds.

# Sea turtle

A sea turtle can live for as long as 100 years! It usually spends its time paddling underwater in warm, shallow seas. Every few years, a mother turtle swims to a sandy beach. She crawls up the shore and lays lots of eggs, which hatch into baby turtles.

A sea turtle swims fast. It uses its long front flippers like oars, as if it is rowing through the water.

At night, a mother turtle digs a hole to lay her **eggs**.

She covers the eggs with sand, using her short **back flippers**.

Huge **front flippers** are great in the water, but they make moving in sand much more difficult.

A thick, heavy **shell** protects the turtle's soft body underneath.

Hard, bony **scales** cover the shell and make it strong.

## It's a fact!

As soon as baby turtles hatch, they climb out of their sandy hole and crawl to the sea. It is an adventure!

It is easy to munch tough seaweed with a sharp **beak**.

 # Shark

A hungry shark swims silently through the water to hunt for its dinner. It can see, hear, and smell a meal from far away. A few kinds of shark, like the great white in the big picture, are fierce, but most are quite shy.

A hammerhead shark looks very odd. It has a wide, flat head like the top of a hammer and an eye at each end.

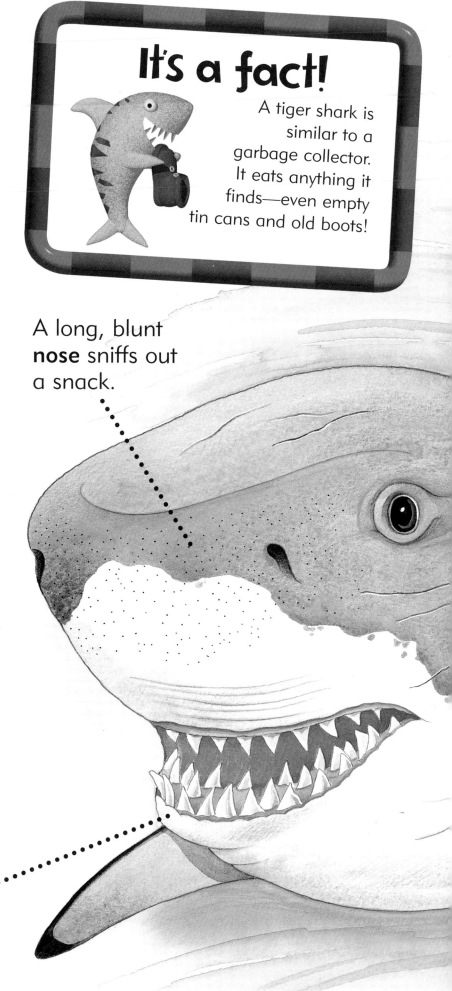

A long, blunt **nose** sniffs out a snack.

Enormous **jaws** snap up even the biggest and strongest fish.

A stiff **fin** helps make it easy to turn in the water.

The **skin** of a shark is very rough.

A shark has rows of razor-sharp teeth. When an old tooth breaks or wears out, a new one takes its place.

A shark pushes itself along by beating its **tail** from side to side.

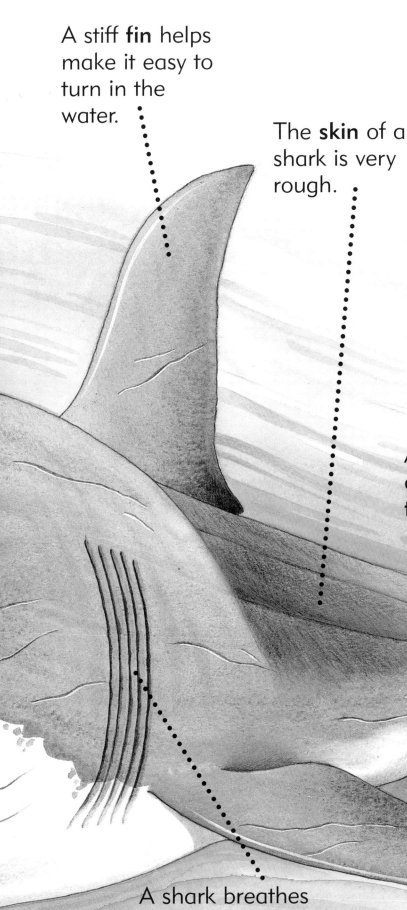

A shark breathes underwater through **gills** on each side of its head.

# Octopus

A slippery octopus spends the day asleep among rocks at the bottom of the ocean. At night, it slithers out of its rocky den to look for tasty food to eat. Most of the time, an octopus crawls across the sea floor, but it's also an excellent swimmer.

An octopus pumps water out of a **funnel** in its body to help it swim.

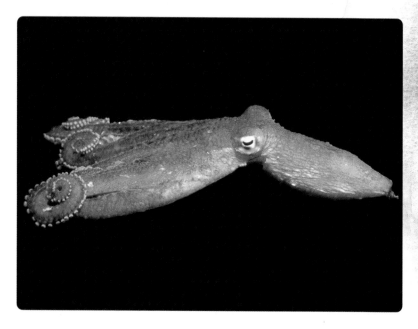

To swim, an octopus stretches its body into a long, thin shape and shoots backward through the water.

It is easy to squeeze into tiny hiding places with a **soft body**.

10

Rows of strong **suckers** help an octopus grip onto rocks.

Can you find an octopus hiding in this picture? Its spotted, orange skin looks as if it is part of the colorful seabed.

A crunchy **crab** makes a juicy meal for a hungry octopus.

An octopus has eight wiggly arms, called **tentacles**.

11

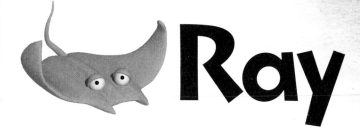 # Ray

Some rays lie on the sandy seabed while others swim near the top of the ocean. In the big picture, you can see a manta ray. Its flat body glides swiftly along like a strange bird. Sometimes it flies right out of the water!

To move, a manta ray flaps its massive **wings** slowly up and down.

Watch out for this spotted stingray. It flicks its spiny, poisonous tail at enemies to give them a nasty sting.

A thin, wispy **tail** trails behind in the water.

A manta ray speeds along so quickly that **small fish** cling on for an exciting ride!

As a manta ray swims, it opens its **mouth** wide to catch tiny creatures.

Two curly **flaps** guide juicy bits the right way.

A manta ray can bend its smooth, **wide body** and do a loop-the-loop!

# It's a fact!

An electric ray has a special way of catching food and defending itself. It stuns fish with electricity from its body so they can't move!

13

# Open ocean

There is plenty of room in the ocean for lots of different animals. They all swim about looking for food to eat.

## Words you know

Here are words that you read earlier in this book. Say them out loud, then try finding the things in the picture.

**gills**      **blowholes**      **tail**

**flippers**    **suckers**      **shell**

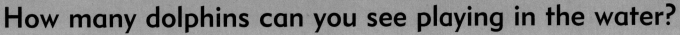

How many dolphins can you see playing in the water?

Which huge animal blows misty spray through its blowholes?

15

Which animal has a soft body and eight wiggly arms?

# Crab

A crab moves sideways on its bony **legs**.

Crabs can be as small as a pea or as big as a dinner plate. They scuttle quickly over the seabed or scurry across the shore. When a dangerous animal comes near, they burrow into the sand or hide under a rock.

Strong **claws** are for crushing food and fighting off attackers.

Eyes on moving **stalks** are good for keeping a look-out!

## It's a fact!

A crab can grow too big for its shell. When it does, the old shell cracks open, leaving a new, larger shell underneath.

A thick, round **shell** protects a crab's back like a coat of armor.

A **flat body** makes it easy to wriggle under rocks.

A hermit crab has no shell of its own. It makes its home in a shell left behind by another creature!

A crab has **feelers** to smell and taste things.

# Colorful fish

Hundreds of colorful fish dart in and out of a coral reef. The water is warm and sunny, and there is plenty to eat. There are also good places to hide from larger creatures that are looking for a meal.

A lionfish scares its enemies away. Red stripes and prickly spines on its body make it look extremely fierce.

**Corals** grow in beautiful shapes and colors.

Slimy **scales** help a fish glide smoothly through the water.

This tuskfish has needle-sharp **teeth** for crunching shellfish.

A **thin body** can slip
easily into narrow
hiding places.

Bright **patterns** make
it hard for an enemy
to spot a fish among
the coral.

To keep safe, these fish swim in a
group, or shoal. It is difficult for an
enemy to tell where one fish ends and
another begins.

# Seahorse

Seahorses are fish that like to bob about gently in seaweed. Seahorses have hundreds of babies. A mother seahorse gives her eggs to a father seahorse. He keeps them all in a special pouch until they hatch.

Bony **rings** protect a seahorse from hungry fish looking for a chewy snack.

A seahorse swims by flapping its tiny **fins** to and fro.

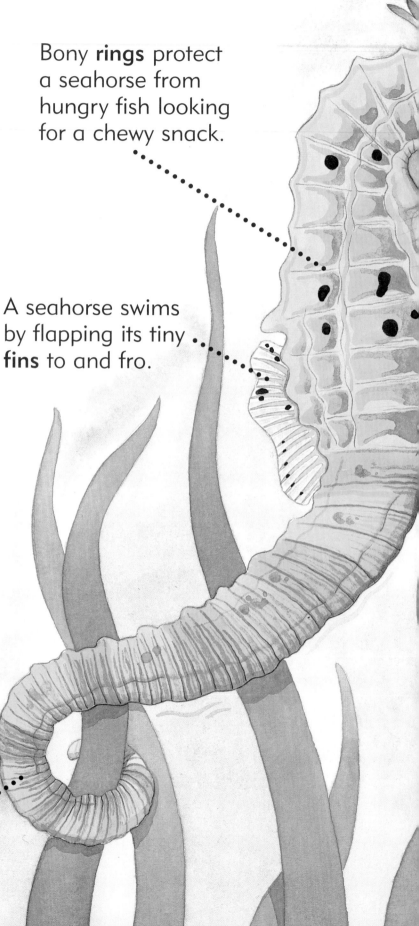

This frilly seahorse has long, leafy fins to trick its enemies. It looks just like a piece of seaweed drifting in the sea!

When a seahorse wants to rest, its curly **tail** is good for clinging onto seaweed.

A seahorse, whose head looks like the head of a tiny horse, sucks up food with its long **snout** and swallows it whole.

Baby seahorses grow inside their father's **pouch** and pop out one after the other.

# It's a fact!

The smallest seahorse in the world is so tiny that it is no taller than a baked bean—that's less than 1 inch (2.5 cm)!

# Unusual creatures

A sea anemone looks like a pretty flower, but this animal traps creatures in its **tentacles** and eats them!

All kinds of unusual creatures cling to the bottom of the sea or drift in the waves. Many of them do not look like animals at all. Each of these creatures has its own clever way of catching food and keeping out of danger.

A round, fleshy **sucker** holds a sea anemone firmly to a rock.

A purple and orange sea slug crawls across the sea floor. Its bright colors warn fish that it tastes horrid!

When a **sea anemone** is scared, it closes up its tentacles and looks like a blob of jelly.

# It's a fact!

A starfish loves to eat shellfish. It wraps its arms around a closed shell and pulls with all its might to reach the tasty food inside.

A **starfish** is shaped like a star. It has five arms covered with small bumps.

You can see right through these jellyfish. Long, stinging tentacles hang beneath their bodies to catch small fish.

A starfish slowly crawls over the seabed on hundreds of little, tubelike **feet**.

# Coral reef

A coral reef is a busy place. How many animals can you find swimming or hiding among the bright corals?

24

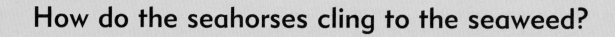

## Words you know

Here are words that you read earlier in this book. Say them out loud, then try finding the things in the picture.

claws    feelers    teeth

fins    tentacles    corals

Which animal has waving tentacles and looks like a flower?

25

# Little Octopus makes new friends

The Octopus family had just moved into Cave Castle,
and Little Octopus felt lonely and homesick.
"I don't like it here. I miss all of my old friends," she sobbed.

Mother Octopus gave her daughter a special octopus cuddle with her long, wiggly tentacles.

"I've been thinking," she said. "We could have a party and invite the neighbors' children so you can make some new friends. It won't be just an ordinary party. It will be a costume party. Then they will all want to come. You can show them your incredible juggling and magic disappearing tricks."

"Oh yes," piped Little Octopus, starting to smile. "That's a great idea!"

Little Octopus sat down to make the party invitations. She found some round, smooth pebbles and decorated the edges with sparkly, gold sand. When the sand was glued on tightly, she wrote in the middle of the pebbles in her best handwriting, using her favorite octopus ink pen. Then she put each pebble inside a pink sea shell and swam off to deliver them to her new neighbors.

Little Crab lived next door to Cave Castle, under a flat, slimy rock. When he saw the bright pink invitation lying on his doorstep, he couldn't wait to find out what was hiding inside. He prodded the shell with his claw to make sure it wouldn't bite, and then carefully opened it.

"I've been invited to a costume party by Little Octopus, who's just moved in next door," he called out to his father. "What am I going to wear?"

"That's easy," chuckled Father Crab. "All we need to do is find a beautiful empty shell. When you climb inside, you'll look like a big, strong hermit crab."

"What a brilliant idea," giggled Little Crab, waving his claws in the air.

So they scuttled to a local second-hand shell shop to find a smart, clean shell.

Little Seahorse lived a little deeper in the sea in a magnificent seaweed garden. When she arrived home from her swimming lesson, she was amazed to see the invitation tangled in the weeds. She opened the shell immediately.

"I've been invited to a costume party by Little Octopus, who's just moved in down the road," she called to her mother. "What am I going to wear?"

"That's easy," replied Mother Seahorse. "I'll sew you a beautiful, frilly dress. When you swim along, you'll look just like a dancing piece of seaweed."

"What a lovely idea," cried Little Seahorse, flapping her tiny fins.

So they swam off to the Deep Ocean Department Store to choose some lacy seaweed and real pearl buttons to make a party dress.

Little Shark lived just around the corner from Cave Castle, in the deep blue ocean.

When he woke from his nap, the pink invitation was bobbing along beside him. Before you could say "snap!" he bit open the shell with his big, jagged teeth.

"I've been invited to a costume party by Little Octopus who's just moved in around the corner," he said to his father. "What am I going to wear?"

"Oh, that's easy," bellowed Father Shark. "All we need to do is find a piece of driftwood in the shape of a hammer. When you tie it to your head, you'll look exactly like a hammerhead shark."

"What a wild idea!" laughed Little Shark, swimming around and around.

So they swam to the top of the ocean to find a piece of floating driftwood that had an unusual shape.

The following morning, all the children were getting ready for the party. Little Crab was shining his shell, Little Seahorse was helping to stitch the last pearl button onto her dress, and Little Shark was painting his hat gray.

Inside Cave Castle, Little Octopus was busy helping her mother sweep the floor and decorate the table with bunches of pretty sea anemones.

In the afternoon, all the creatures rushed excitedly over to Cave Castle to meet Little Octopus. They had never been inside an octopus's home before.

Little Octopus was waiting at the entrance to the cave. She had turned bright purple to match the door and was

the lovely food in one mouthful!

After they had feasted, Little Octopus put on a special magic show. She made herself disappear behind a cloud of black octopus ink and reappear in a different part of the cave. Then she juggled with nine tiny, painted pebbles. Everyone clapped loudly. They all wished they had eight long tentacles, too.

When it was time to go home, the children thanked Little Octopus for the best party in the ocean.

"You must come and see us tomorrow in our favorite adventure playground. We'll play hide-and-seek," they all said excitedly. "We'll wait for you in front of the big spotted rock."

"I'll be there," said Little Octopus, as she waved good-by.

The next day Little Octopus woke up bright and early.

"I know what I'll do," she smiled. "If I hide in the playground before they arrive, then I can surprise them all again with my magic tricks."

So Little Octopus rushed to the playground and changed the color of her skin to match the spotted rock. "They'll

wearing a tiny golden crown on her head.

"I'm so pleased you could make it," sang Little Octopus, twirling her arms like a windmill and shooting up to the ceiling. "Do come in."

The inside of the cave was more beautiful than any of them had imagined. There were red and orange starfish clinging to the black stone walls and glowing jellyfish lanterns floating near the ceiling. The table was piled high with delicious golden sandburgers, spiky seaweed salad, blue sea salt crisps, and multicolored coral cakes.

Little Shark was on his best behavior and had to stop himself from eating all

never see me now," she giggled.

When Little Crab, Little Seahorse, and Little Shark arrived, they waited for Little Octopus in front of the big spotted rock.

"I wonder where she is?" said Little Crab, peering behind some seaweed.

"I hope she turns up soon," said Little Seahorse, tapping her fins.

"Maybe she's decided not to come after all," said Little Shark, tossing his head.

"Here I am!" shouted Little Octopus.

All the animals turned around to look at the big spotted rock, but they couldn't see anyone.

Little Octopus waved her tentacles and the rock looked as if it was moving.

"Wow!" gasped Little Crab. "Is that you, Little Octopus?"

Little Octopus blushed and her skin turned red, so she wasn't hidden anymore.

"We're so pleased you're here," sighed Little Seahorse. "It's been such fun since you moved into Cave Castle. There are so many games we want to play with you, but not hide-and-seek. You're far too good at that."

"Come on everyone," whistled Little Shark, as he started to swim away. "Catch me if you can!"

"I guess I'm not going to be lonely here after all," thought Little Octopus, smiling at her new friends.

# Puzzles

## Double trouble!

These two pictures of sea creatures look the same, but they aren't. Can you find four differences?

**a**

**b**

## Close-up!

We've zoomed in on parts of animals that you have seen in this book. Can you figure out who they belong to?

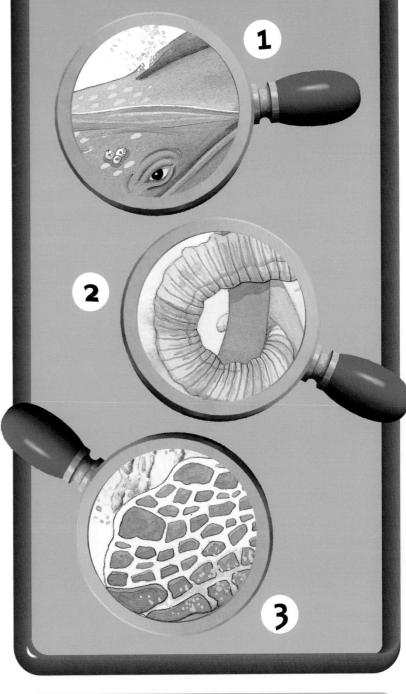

1

2

3

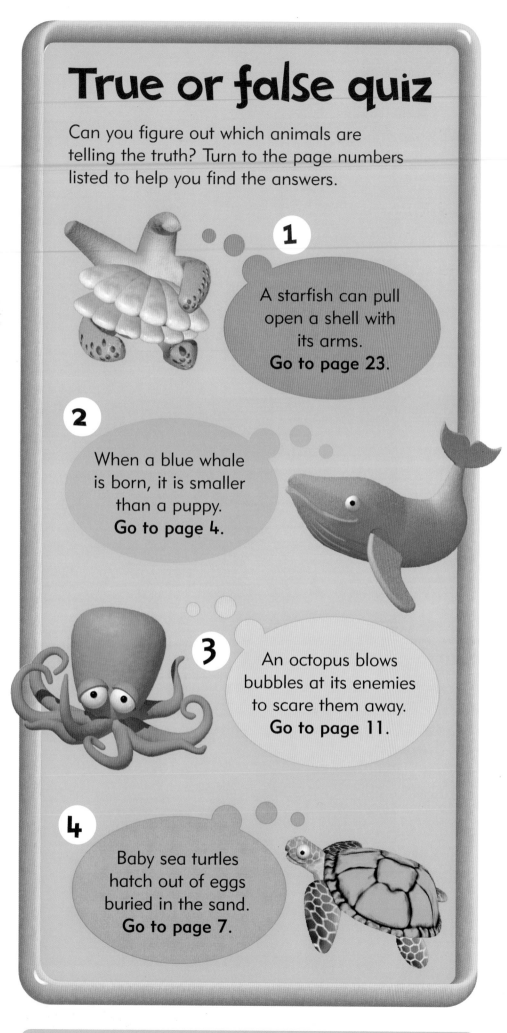

# True or false quiz

Can you figure out which animals are telling the truth? Turn to the page numbers listed to help you find the answers.

**1**

A starfish can pull open a shell with its arms.
**Go to page 23.**

**2**

When a blue whale is born, it is smaller than a puppy.
**Go to page 4.**

**3**

An octopus blows bubbles at its enemies to scare them away.
**Go to page 11.**

**4**

Baby sea turtles hatch out of eggs buried in the sand.
**Go to page 7.**

Answers: 1 true, 2 false, 3 false, 4 true.

# Index